Packer Poems & Punchlines

Green & Gold Gags to Make You
(Lambeau) Leap With Laughter!

Other products from Edelstein Productions, LLC:

- **The Packer Fan(atic) Handbook: Jokes, Barbs, Fun & Facts**
  (Badger Books)

- **Packer Punchlines Radio Show**
  (in development)

- **Packer humor products**
  (online store products; in development)

Edelstein Productions, LLC
12 Kingfisher Avenue
Novato, CA 94949
415-382-1827
877-425-9106

packerjokes.com
info@packerjokes.com

Packer Poems & Punchlines

Green & Gold Gags to Make You
(Lambeau) Leap With Laughter!

by Mike Marn

Packer Poems & Punchlines:
Green & Gold Gags to Make You (Lambeau) Leap With Laughter!

An Edelstein Productions, LLC book / eBook / Second Edition 2017

Author: *Mike Marn*

Cover Design: *Jim Hunt*
jimhunt.us

Inside Cartoons:
Jim Haynes, Graphics Plus
jimhaynes@verizon.net, 240-997-9612, naddydaddy.etsy.com
https://www.facebook.com/pages/Graphics-Plus-Inc/181609428554884?ref=hl
&
Tom Tomasz "the12" Stasiak
http://thetwelve-matsujama12.blogspot.com

Library of Congress Cataloging-in-Publication Data

Marn, Mike
Packer Poems & Punchlines:
Green & Gold Gags to Make You (Lambeau) Leap With Laughter / Mike Marn

ISBN 978-0997145601
PRINTED IN THE UNITED STATES OF AMERICA
OPM 0 9 8 7

Table of Contents

Introduction

These poems are just an expression,
Of a Packer fan's crazy obsession.
You'll find that they rhyme,
Nearly all of the time.
(But sometimes they don't — a confession.)

"We hope you like at least 65.4% of them, so we can beat A-Rod's career completion percentage."*

(* = at time of publishing. Hopefully, it's higher now.)

Archrivals & Enemies:

NFC North

B

The "Monsters of the Midway" like to think of themselves as the Packers' big rival. More correct, in recent years, the Bears typically hibernate when playing Green Bay.

No matter. Ditka and the 1986 Super Bowl team are still beloved. Trouble is, most fans have misplaced their history books.

Thirty years is a long time — and a great reason to rhyme.

Bears (are) History!

Bears fans talk about the past,
No surprise — they gotta.
Since 1986, "success"
they haven't had a lotta.

Even then, their biggest star,
was a "Refrigerator."
His bulk struck fear in everyone:
Teammates, foes, and waiters!

Bears fans get new hope for glory,
Each and every year.
But by December, they'll be looking
In their rear view mirror.

"Did I do that?"
BEARS ROOKIES:
FLATTENED "BUSTS"
PERRY
72

De-clawed Bears

We've all been warned to fear the bear.
"Be careful in the forest,"
'Just keep your distance. Stay away!"
"Maybe they'll ignore us."

To Packer fans, the danger seems
A trifle over-stated.
The Bears that come to Lambeau
Are de-clawed and over-rated.

An EmBEARassing Limerick

Bear fans bellow their ignorant cheers
In their Triple X parkas from Sears.
If you want to have fun,
Tell 'em they haven't won
The Big One in 31 years.

QB Hall of Shame Limerick

Our QBs are all Hall-of-Famers,
But in Chi-town, they're quite a bit lamer.
They come and they go,
'Cuz they can't make a throw.
And we're hoping for more of the samer.

Rivalry? Yeah, Right.

The Bears like to call us a "rival."
But for them, it's a fight for survival.
We fill them with fear.
(Beat them **THREE TIMES** one year.)
In Lambeau, they're dead on arrival.

A Career Heading South (Again)

When at last, they said "adios, Jay."
Bears fans were giddy all day.
He went briefly to Fox,
But much to our shock,
The Dolphins think he can still play!

ObamaCare vs. Obama's Bears

Former President Obama and "ObamaCare" have become love/hate legends. So have his hometown Bears. Let's see what they have in common.

Obama and ObamaCare	Obama's Bears
More people got medical coverage.	Bears QB's need more medical coverage, thanks to leaky offensive line.
Spent four years living in an old building provided by the taxpayers.	Still play in an old building provided by the taxpayers.
For Vice Presidency, it was "Biden time."	Always Bidin' time, waiting for next year's draft.
Spoke in clipped tones to get points across.	Opponents often clipped and held, stopping Bears from crossing the goal line to score.
Won twice in eight years.	Actually did better than that. A little.
Hiked taxes, frustrating many Americans.	Hike footballs, with results usually taxing to their fans.

We're Bringing Out the Fine Cutlery

It's always great to make fun of the Bears QB play over the past twenty-some years.Or, more correctly stated: the Bears' ABSENCE of QB play in recent seasons.

Consider the night-and-day contrast between the Bears and Packers QB play from the early 1990s until today. The Packers' two superstar QBs — Brett Favre and Aaron Rodgers (the former a Hall of Famer and the latter a future shoe-in) — contrast with the Bears' lengthy list of mostly forgettable signal callers.

In fact, imagine holding a list of infamous Bears QBs in recent years. It would reach the floor. They've had more QB busts than Canton. But one name stands out as the most erratic, most inconsistent, and most frustrating of all.
Can you guess? It's an easy pick: Jay Cutler..........or, more apt, easy picks — given Jay threw a whopping 23 interceptions vs. the Packers when playing for the Bears.

Indeed, as testimony to Jay Cutler's inglorious failures vs. the Packers, after yet another loss to the Green & Gold, the Packers' Charles Woodson said in the locker room: "Same Old Jay."

Woodson would have been equally correct in noting Bears fans will be glad to forget the Jay Cutler era in Chicago ever occurred. His infamous legacy upon initially retiring in 2017 at age 33? He won merely two of 14 contests in his career vs. Green Bay.

But wait: the story gets even stranger. After the Bears finally cut him, he took a job a Fox analyst. But before he could call a game, he was lured out of retirement by $10 million from the Miami Dolphins, who will now have their own "Jay Cutler era." Bottom line, if you want to see dolphins, go to Sea World. You're not likely to see them in the NFL playoffs anytime soon.

Not with the "same old Jay."

So, Jay, the following limerick and "news items" are dedicated to you. From all us Packer fans: "Thanks for the memories!":

Moan Over Miami

Whenever you asked his Bears teammates,
They always said all the right things.
Jay's got a great arm, he's a leader.
But with him they never won rings.

He has a great arm, that's for certain,
But he threw lots of picks in the clutch.
He may be the best in Bears' history.
But let's face it — that's not saying much.

Now he's down in the land of Marino,
Who was one of the best of all time.
Fans had best not get excited.
Ten million bucks for Jay is a crime.

News items about Jay:

- After his release by Chicago (but BEFORE he returned to the NFL), free agent Jay Cutler was asked if he would play for the Packers if anything happened to Aaron Rogers. He replied "I'd probably have to pass."

  Comment: Good decision. Anything requiring him to pass is probably not going to end well.

- Reporters pressed further: "But what if Rogers was hurt and the Packers called?" Cutler still said "I'm probably not going to do it."

  Comment: What a shame. Given his success at throwing to players wearing Packers jerseys, you would think Jay would quickly feel comfortable (i.e., Jay's infamous epitaph vs. Green Bay: an all-time record of 2-12 and 23 interceptions).

- Before he was lured back to the NFL, Jay signed with Fox Sports as its new "color" man for NFL telecasts.

  Comment: Jay's glad his great scrambling ability included quitting from the job before it began by using the protection of an escape clause to return to the NFL. That security blanket worked better than his offensive line's protection in Chicago —given he was sacked a whopping 251 times in just seven seasons there.

- Some media wrote that the poor body language and apparent disinterest Cutler showed on the field made him ill-suited for a "color analyst" job.

  Comment: When asked if that could be a problem, Cutler shrugged his shoulders and said "whatever."

- On his first day of returning to the NFL, Jay Cutler was confused as to why dozens of opposing players welcomed him back with the words: "Many happy returns."

  Comment: Jay forgot he has thrown 18 "pick six" interceptions returned for touchdowns in his career through 2016 — one of which former Packer Casey Hayward returned 82 yards for a touchdown during a 55-14 Packer romp over the Bears in 2014

V

Yup, there IS a place colder than Lambeau. At least it feels that way to frustrated Vikings fans — year after year. Let's count the ways: legal troubles, ownership woes, and stadium battles. Heck, they even fired their mascot. Plus, the revolving door at quarterback NEVER seems to stop spinning.

Maybe things are looking up with Teddy Bridge-Over-Troubled-Water (hopefully recovering from ACL surgery) and Sam "Healthy Half the Time" Bradford. And if things get really desperate, we can offer them the phone number of an old friend in Mississippi who might be willing to help. Meanwhile, read below, because when it comes to poems, the Vikings are a stanza bonanza!

Missed It by THAT Much

If the Super Bowl's not to your liking,
You should be a fan of the Vikings.

Just when it looked like they'd won,
Old Brett threw a pick — they were done.

In 1998, looked like they'd won,
But a kick went wide left. They were done.

Against the Seahawks, one kick to win...
But a gimme is missed once again.

One year, when the critics all raved,
The roof on their Metrodome caved!

Their QB finally seemed ready.
But an injury took out poor Teddy.

Are they FINALLY making some gains?
Nah — those Super Bowl dreams? Down the drain!

4

Hornless Vikings

"Vikings" — ahh, it makes you think of
Warriors bringing thunder,
Ruthless Norsemen, charging forth
To pillage and to plunder.

To Packer fans, however,
Vikings just aren't world beaters.
They're usually down by 20,
Warming hands on sideline heaters.

Back To The Future For The Vikes

It's always a pretty good bet,
That with talent, the Vikings are set.
Except at QB,
Where WHO KNOWS what you'll see!
A raw rookie — or past-his-prime Brett!

The Vikings New "U.S. Bank Stadium"

Have the Vikings put lipstick on a pig-skin palace? Their new stadium cost $1.13 billion, but we don't blame them. With the teams they usually trot out, you'd better distract the fans with SOMETHING. Let's take a look at some special facts about this obscene, ostentatious monument to wretched excess.

A Glass Ceiling

They saved a little money by skipping the retractable roof. But it's not all bad — this way when frustrated fans look to the heavens in frustration, they'll have a better view. Another plus: they're hoping that if the roof ever caves in like the Metrodome did, you won't notice because it's glass — and it won't go as viral as the last one did.

Naming Rights

U.S. Bancorp paid $212 million for naming rights to the stadium for the next 20 years. Customers need not worry, however — it's not like any banks ever got into any trouble for making sketchy investments in the last decade or anything.

The Fan Experience

The amenities are amazing, like a costly new in-stadium smartphone app that will tell you where the shortest concession and bathroom lines are. A better idea? How about simply spending more money to build additional concession stands and bathrooms. Also, the closest seats to the field are only 41 feet away from the action. That's a great view of the action — but better stay alert, given the accuracy shown by recent Viking QBs and placekickers.

A Versatile Venue

Developers say the cost of the stadium is reasonable and "worth it" to the community, especially because it will also host entertainment events, soccer games, and, even, WWE matches. No word yet as to whether there are plans to get an actual professional football team to play in it.

LIONS

Ah, the Silver and Honolulu Blue. A North Division rival, the Lions and their fans have been mostly blue in recent years: Who will ever forget the team's perfectly imperfect 0-16 season in 2011? You can't do any worse — so that certainly calls for verse!

Music Motown = Football NO-town

Records from Detroit are great.
The music scene is cool!
Great *football* records? Not so much.
A fan feels like a fool.

Motown, rap, and hip-hop
Are the local styles preferred.
But from the mouths of Lions' fans,
Only blues are heard.

LOSERS
FORD FIELD
blues
dandeLIONS

A Limerick That Sure Ain't Lyin'

The Lions act like they're the best.
Their defense presents quite a test.
But we're happy to say
That their stars seldom play.
Often, they're under arrest.

Titletown, USA

Detroit is on the rise, they say.
(Their record doesn't show it.)
Vikings? Hey, they're coming back!
(Relax – they always blow it.)

The Bears new coach has fans abuzz,
but hasn't helped their play.
So when the dust has cleared,
Division champs will be Green Bay.

Tame Lions

"*Lions*" — yikes, the jungle king.
A creature we should fear.
Surely we must quiver if
We ever see him near.

But Packer fans? We stand our ground.
Just let those Lions roar.
A few years back, they didn't win a *game.*
(Not sure they scored!)

The Lions "Coaching Tree"

These days, there's a lot of talk about "coaching trees" — where one successful coach "breeds" respected assistants who get head coaching jobs of their own.

In fact, if there was a tree planted in downtown Detroit sprouting all the Lions head coaches since 1988 — well, it might be time to call a tree service.

Just look at these **SAP**-lings:

Coach	Years	Record With Lions
Fontes	1988-96	66-67
Ross	1997-2000	27-30
Moeller	2000	4-3
Mornhinweg	2001-02	5-27
Mariucci	2003-05	15-28
Jauron	2005	1-4
Marinelli	2006-08	10-38
Schwartz	2009-13	29-51
Caldwell	2014 - ?	18-14

Some coaching tree. Must be a **DOG**wood.

Other Archrivals We Love to ~~Hate~~

Dislike

Cowboys

They say everything is larger in Texas. Obviously, it's true: Jerry Jones' ego, the constant Cowboys' hype, and Dallas fans' huge disappointment over their annual .500 or below record.

America's team? They might be America's meme. They think they're great, but the results don't show it. And that kind of thing can inspire a poet. (Get it? THAT was a little poem right there.)

Why Send a CowBOY to Do a General Manager's Job?

A bank teller that just couldn't add?
Or a butcher that just couldn't cut it?
A mechanic who didn't know how a car works?
A golfer who just couldn't putt it?

Must be okay with the Cowboys, though.
To keep a GM who can't manage.
TWO playoff wins since '97?
Being owner is quite an advantage.

No Mo' Romo

On paper, every year it seems
The Cowboys ought to win it.
But once you see the injured list
You'd best hold off a minute.

Dez Bryant has a foot that hurts
(and knee, and leg, and more).
And every week, new injuries
Claim players by the score.

Romo missed so many games,
He finally had to quit.
Prescott filled in nicely, but
We cringed with every hit.

The Cowboys aren't so scary
With all back-ups in the game.
But Tony? Hope you wind up
In the I.R. Hall of Fame.

Dallas Cowboy Leer-Leaders

They twirl and strut and prance and cheer
their way across the field.
White high-heeled boots and cleavage
Add some flash and sex appeal.

Ever wonder why their skirts
get shorter every year?
Distracted fans don't boo as much —
and buy a lot more beer.

GIANTS

The Giants recent playoff success against the Pack? Well earned, with Super Bowl rings the result. But that was then. Now, with Eli at the helm, the Giants have a way of shooting themselves in the foot (not talking about you, Plaxico). So it's time they faced a little poetic justice.

Sofa, So Good.

The Packers won
A championship in 1961.
We scored 37 points,
The Giants? Sadly, none.

Alas, they're sad again today.
The playoffs are quite rare.
And even when they make it,
It's the Packers waiting there.

Is Eli getting old? Is it the coach?
It's hard to tell.
All I know is if they were a stock,
I'd holler "SELL!"

Respect, Yes. Games, No.

They've got themselves a couple rings,
Not fair to call 'em slackers.
But the "Giants" aren't so big,
When they take on the Packers.

Eli, as a quarterback
just isn't quite elite.
When the Packer D's around,
He's just not hard to beat.

"AARON, GREAT SUPER BOWL WIN!"
"THANKS, HOPE MY GIANT BUDDIES ENJOYED WATCHING FROM HOME!"

Manning the Lifeboats

Let's meet two famous brothers,
Both QB's, extraordinaire.
They piled up lots of stats,
But big wins were pretty rare.

If PEYTON was your favorite,
Then you had a lot to cheer.
An ocean full of passing stats.
A Hall of Fame career.

But if your favorite's ELI,
His record's also decent.
His Giants won a couple rings,
(But nothing very recent.)

Peyton finally hung it up,
though he didn't want to go.
Eli's getting pretty close,
But doesn't seem to know.

49ERS

When fans think of the San Francisco 49ers, their minds wander to the team's previous golden age when Joe Montana, Steve Young and Jerry Rice earned Lombardi Trophies. Then the team went south for few years.

More recently, the team's glory days returned, but that success turned out to be fool's gold — and all the fans got was the shaft. So to add a dose of reality. . . the pleasure is all, uh — mine!

49ers Not Panning Out

Harbaugh had the Niners
going well for several years.
But then his style wore pretty thin —
he left, and few shed tears.

His ego and his temper
caused a lot of inside rifts,
But since he left for Michigan,
the team has been adrift.

Several stars have walked away,
signed elsewhere, or been traded.
The dynasty is done, we fear —
the glory has all faded.

49
49

Gold Rushing the Wrong Way

The Forty-Niners used to be
the height of class and style.
But that was way back when they won —
And it's been quite a while.

Montana, Young, and Jerry Rice,
The roster once was loaded.
With Hall of Famers everywhere.
But now, things have eroded.

The stars have all been traded,
And the famous coach is history.
Where the QB's talent went
Remains a puzzling mystery.

But one thing's true, no matter what.
When they take on the Pack.
A win's not gonna happen
Unless Rice and Young come back!

SEAHAWKS

The Seahawks have Russelled up some success lately, creating a legend of invincibility. But their rise was in part fueled by the Fail Mary play in 2012, when replays showed one Packer DB was interfered with and another intercepted the final long pass.

Moral of the story? The overmatched replacement official who allowed the game-winning touchdown to stand was, obviously, Seattle's first "12th Man."

Sleepiness in Seattle

The Seahawks were the story
Just a few short years ago.
Seattle was the place that
Rivals hated most to go.

It was noisy, it was hostile
And the players dominated.
The running back was "Beast Mode."
It was talking that he hated.

The team was best remembered
For the atitude it showed.
When Richard Sherman barked to the media
His angry feelings really flowed.

But ever since the dopey goal line call
Cost a Super Bowl win,
The Seahawks haven't been the same.
It's quite a fix they're in.

Beast Mode's gone, and Sherman
Doesn't' screech as loud these days.
Guess no one wants to hear you talk
If you're not making plays.

Seahawks or ME-hawks?

The Seahawks seem so nasty,
with their brash intimidation.
They trash-talk foes, and even
ladies from the TV station.

They love to be on camera,
And hype that "12th man" stuff.
It's kinda sad, because for us,
Eleven is enough.

Emerald City Slickers – A Limerick

If you're partial to trash talk and hype,
Then the Seahawks are surely your type.
Just remember one game,
Was a sham, and a shame.
"Fail Mary" was hogwash and tripe.

Packer Nation & Titletown Muse

PACKERS

We saved the best for last: the finest team, the heartiest fans, the most venerable stadium, and the smartest owners in the league — all 360,760 Packer fans who own stock in the team.

In recent years, success for the Pack was earned despite injuries and other tough patches. In other words (and with apologies to Charles Dickens) it was the best of rhymes, it was the worst of rhymes.

PACK RULES!

PACKERS — THE PLAYERS

Don't Cut the Cheese, A-Rod!

Aaron, a word with you, please?
You know that we love you, but JEEZE!
Our hearts were deflated
When news reports stated
That you said you wouldn't eat CHEESE!

As quarterback, you are a master.
Of the green-and-gold flock, you're the pastor.
But those horrible words, chilled us down to our curds!
It's truly a dairy disaster.

No small cubes of swiss or of cheddar?
And no provolone? That's no better.
No cheese at your parties? Not even havarti?
Those parties just couldn't be deader.

Pizza needs cheese, so *that's* out.
And tacos are gone too, no doubt.
Your dinners must suck. Want great taste? Out of luck.
NO CHEESE?! (Sorry, don't mean to shout.)

So Aaron, we beg you, don't do it.
Just pile on the cheese — nothing to it!
On the field, you can hear it.
Make a touchdown, we cheer it.
What WE make is CHEESE — don't eschew it.

Mauled by Matthews

"The ball was snapped; I saw a hole.
I really did, I swear.
But after two quick steps I found
It was no longer there.
The wall I hit was sheer concrete!
(At least, it felt that way.)
But soon I learned that I was wrong —
'Twas really made of Clay!"

52
CLAY
MAKER

Made in Wisconsin

Brett was better in Green Bay,
Than anywhere he played.
Matt Flynn stunk with other teams,
But WE sure got him paid.

A-Rod's played for no one else,
So who can really say?
Turns out our QB string ain't LUCK —
It's here QB's are MADE!

4
4
DEANNA
Packers
Hall Of Fame
?
12
12
MVP
12
MOM
OLIVIA

The Life of Riley RODGERS

They say that Aaron's got it all,
Hard to disagree.
Seems like things have gone his way,
Let's just look at THREE:

Drafted by the Packers, he
got to learn from Brett.
With the stats he piling up now,
the Hall's a darned good bet.

His social life? It's not too bad,
with rich and famous friends.
Attractive women wait for him,
Nearby when each game ends.

He goes on Jeopardy and makes
the others look like slackers.
A jock with brains? It isn't FAIR!
At least he's with the Packers.

A "Just Leave" Limerick

Lately when they leave Green Bay,
ex-Packers have lots to say!
Not sure why they're carin'
about us or Aaron
instead of their own crappy play.

Putting the ER in PackERs

In recent years the injuries
Have hit us hard. Oh, Lordy!
They've knocked out our bygone greats: Lacy, Cook, and Shields.
Twice, they've cost us Jordy!

But Packer fans keep the faith.
We may have ups and downs,
No matter WHAT we suffer through,
At least we're not the Browns.

PACKERS — THE FANS

A Packer Fan Pick Six

Home wins are almost a lock,
since our "guests" find the weather a shock.
But our fans are the thing
that will give us the ring.
They not only cheer, they own STOCK.

SECTION ROW SEAT
09 57 22
ANNUAL STOCKHOLDER
MEETING
You're Invited
BYOB
(BRING YOUR
OWN BRATS)
USE STADIUM ENT
P2
PRICE
SECTION
09
SEAT
22

"What Cold?" Tundra Man Says

Heartier fans you won't find.
Rain, sleet, or snow we don't mind.
A blizzard predicted?
We're just not conflicted.
We'll be there the usual time.

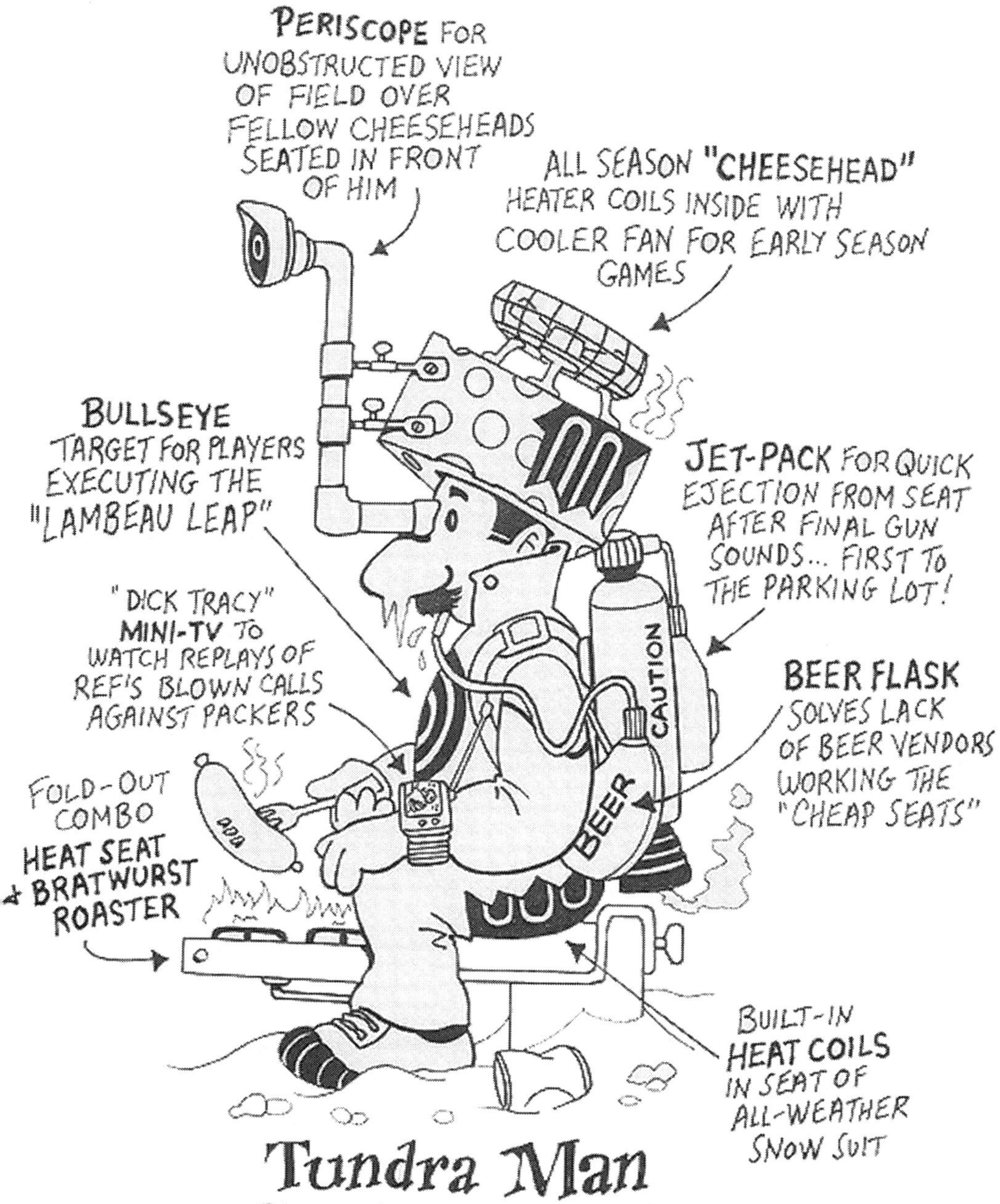

Tundra Man

(GREENBAYIS PACKERIS)

TD Celebration: Packer Style

Packer fans don't act like sheep.
We're feisty, and make others weep!
Don't mean to be rude,
But if you don't like our 'tude,
Take a flying (but not Lambeau) leap!

"Hey, Beer Man!"

Some look at Green Bay and they sneer.
Think we come 'cause there's nothing else here!
That there's nothing to do,
But that's not at all true.
We could always stay home and drink beer.

PACK
PACK RULES
GO!
PACK ATTACK
LOVE THAT PACK!
GO PACK
HEY! BEER MAN

Packer Fan Fashion

Cheeseheads? That's kind of old hat.
So we'd rather you not call us that.
And we'd rather not see
Ourselves on TV,
'Cause our butt-warmers make us look fat!

Packer Fans: Ice Bowl Tough

When we heard of a movie called "Frozen"
We all started strutting and posing,
How could it not feature
It just *had* to feature
Our frost-covered kiesters!
But *no* – the *wrong* story was chosen.

Pack the Pick of the Litter

Every year, our rivals
In the rugged North Division,
Spend sleepless nights preparing
For their one and only mission.

When interviewed, they'll say
They want to win the Super Bowl.
Don't believe it. It's not true.
They have a simpler goal.

The prize that they want most in life,
The thing of which they dream
Is winning once, against the Pack.
And so, each year they scheme.

The Vikings tried a new QB,
And famous running back.
But no matter what they do,
They seldom beat the Pack.

The Bears brought in new coaches,
To help Cutler get it done.
Now Jay is gone, and so is hope.
For fans, it's not much fun.

The Lions start out hopeful,
Their quarterback can throw it.
But no one on the roster scares the Pack.
(I'm sure they know it.)

As for us, we're loaded, and
With A-Rod in command,
It seems to us the title
Still is safely in our hands.

VIKINGS
PSL FUND
$$?

Hunting — But What Game?

The time of year we hate the most
Is when we have to choose,
Just where to freeze our tushies off,
Enjoying friends and booze.

It's hunting season, so we must
decide; it's such a shame.
Drop a buck right in his tracks?
Or hundreds on the game!

We always choose the Packers,
for touchdowns, picks, and sacks.
"Cause after all, the deer camp will
be there when we get back.

And things we hear at Lambeau,
are sure to help us cope:
the "shotgun" snap, "the refs are blind"
and "kill the clock, you dope!"

So late November, find us
in the woodlots, stalking deer.
But we'll be back by game time,
Packer Nation — never fear!

Lambeau Legacy

From the days of Donny, Vince, and Bart,
To A-Rod, Cobb, and Clay,
The Packers have stood tall and proud,
From past, to present day.
No matter who wears Green and Gold,
The outcome's not a mystery.
In Lambeau, foes take on a piece
Of living, breathing history.

Packers' All-time Great

To pick the greatest Packer?
A thankless task, for sure.
So many legends long ago,
So many stars, much newer.

Historic names roll off the tongue,
And Bart is near the top.
A Starr, indeed, there's no debate.
You think he's not? Oh, STOP.

And heading up the "D" back then,
One guy led the way.
Nitschke caused opponents fear,
And his name is fun to say!

But there were lots of other greats.
Adderly, Jordan, Davis.
No, THAT defense would never rest.
Opponents yelled, 'Lord, save us!"

On offense, Hornung had a ball,
And carried it like crazy.
And Taylor in the backfield, too?
That left opponents hazy.

Along the way, some others came,
All surely Packer greats.
Think Kramer, White, and Woodson,
Sterling Sharpe, and Lofton. WAIT!

This list could last FOREVER. Can't limit it to codgers.
Brett Farve is near the top himself! (And so is Aaron Rodgers.)

And what of good-hands Jordy?
Where does Clay Matthews fit?
So many big-name players!
I guess that's the fun of it.

In the end, I'm glad that I
Don't have to be the picker.
The list's already far too long,
(And that's not counting kickers!)

The most exciting thing about
This all-time Packers' great?
What if we haven't SEEN him yet?
We fans can hardy wait!

Vince-sanity

A fiery coach from years ago,
Made one thing very clear:
Winning's all that matters — and
We've always shown that here.

He wouldn't stand for tricky plays,
Or fancy touchdown dances.
His QB's had to toe the line
And not take many chances.

Sure, Bart would throw a bomb
On 3rd and one, and sometimes hit it.
But Vince would rather send a back
Right through the line and get it.

His language was a little rough
From time to time, it's true.
But what the ____ *was* going on out there?
I didn't know. Did *you*?

Lombardi told it like it was.
His players loved him for it.
His passion for the game so strong,
That *no one* could ignore it.

Vince was always colorful,
Determined, and demanding.
That's why the trophy *named* for him
Goes to the last team standing.

Leaders Of The Pack

Every year, our rivals in
the NFC North division.
have something up their collective sleeves
to help achieve their mission.

They tell reporters that they want
To reach the Super Bowl.
But deep down we all know
Their one and only goal.

The thing that they want most in life
The thing of which they dream,
Is winning games against the Pack.
And so, each year, they scheme.

The Vikings put a lot of faith
In their new quarterback.
But that won't get the "W" —
Go try another tack!

The Bears are putting stock, instead,
In their new batch of coaches.
But we're not scared, 'cause at the line,
Glennon or Trubisky still approaches.

The Lions are a puzzling bunch.
Their fans can't be inspired.
Their Hall of Fame receiver's
pretty young — but he retired.

The Pack? We've still got all our studs,
With Aaron in command.
Seems to us that we've still got
The title in our hands.

A Warm Wisconsin Welcome (Sort Of)

Out-of-staters, welcome!
We'd love to see you here.
We're famous for our cheeses
And our legendary beer.

Enjoy our rolling countryside,
and forests tall and green,
The people are the friendliest
You've probably ever seen.

From Minnesota, Michigan, or
Illinois? That's great!
Stay the weekend, stay a week.
Our businesses can't wait.

Take home some swiss or cheddar.
Our sausage can't be topped.
Plus quilts and crafty items from
our quaint and cozy shops.

But still we have to warn you,
If you've come to play the Pack.
Sadness is the souvenir
You're likely taking back.

Attention, Pack and Packer fans,
here's YOUR part of the poem:
If they show up at Lambeau Field
Just beat 'em — send 'em home.

The Aaron Rodgers Radio Show

Featuring host Aaron Rodgers
& his (infamous) guests

GUEST: MATT FLYNN

AARON: Back again with "Aaron on the Air." I'm Aaron Rodgers, and let's take some more calls. Who's this waiting on the line? Hello?

FLYNN: Hey, Aaron, it's your old buddy....

AARON: Uh, hi....and your name, caller?

FLYNN: Aaron, it's me! Matt Flynn?

AARON: Matt Flynn, Matt Flynn — uh, did we hang out in high school?

FLYNN: No, Aaron — it's Matt Flynn, your backup with the Packers a few years back.

AARON: Oh, yes, now I remember. Started for me a couple times when I was injured?

FLYNN: Yeah, surely you remember? — I threw for 480 yards and six touchdowns in ONE GAME!

AARON: Sure, but that was against the Lions, right? That doesn't count. Everyone does. But anyway, what's been going on?

FLYNN: Well, I bounced around after I left Green Bay. But I was backup QB for some big names..... like Terrell Pryor...

AARON: He doesn't even play quarterback any more.

FLYNN: And Luke McCown, and Jeff Tuel...

AARON: Who?

FLYNN: I even backed up Tom Brady. Well, I backed up the guy who backed up Tom Brady. Anyway, I'm looking for work again. Could you put in a word for me? I'd sure like to come back to the Packers again!

AARON: Uh, sorry, Matt. I think they're looking to bring in Johnny Manziel.

Mystery Caller

AARON: Hello, caller, welcome to Aaron on the Air. What's on your mind?

KJ: Uh...yeah, Aaron, you have a lot of nerve.

AARON: Huh? Who IS this?

KJ: Ken Jennings. You know, the ALL TIME Jeopardy champ? The guy who won 74 straight times on that show and won over $3 million?

AARON: Yeah, okay, I remember you. So, why are you calling?

KJ: Well, do I come in to Lambeau Field and start throwing touchdown passes and make you look ordinary?

AARON: No, but...

KJ: Do I march in for a day like some prima donna and make it look easy to move it down the field and beat the other team?

AARON: Well, no, but you couldn't.

KJ: Do I sneak in and perform so well the fans and TV announcers forget about YOU, like you made Alex Trebek forget about me?

AARON: No, it's a totally different game, and. . .

KJ: Ha! That's it, Rodgers, you LOSE. I asked you three questions, and none of your responses were in the form of a question. (MAKES BUZZER NOISE.) You lose. Ha!

AARON: Sure, whatever.

KJ: No, that's "what IS whatever" — loser!

SFX: CLICK. (KJ HANGS UP)

AARON: What is.... a moron? Next caller.

Special Guest: Vince

AARON: Hello, I'm Aaron Rodgers and we're back with Aaron on the Air. Let's go this week's first caller, and I'm told it's Vince. Go ahead, Vince, what's on your mind?

VINCE: (GRUFF) Yeah, I wanna know what the hell's going on up there?

AARON: Excuse me?

VINCE: WHAT THE HELL'S GOING ON UP THERE?

AARON: This sure sounds like — Vince? Vince LOMBARDI? Is that YOU?

VINCE: Damn right it's me. I just heard you guys lost THREE STRAIGHT GAMES. So what the hell is going on up there?

AARON: Well, the league is tough, sir, and it's not easy to win. Every team goes through a rough patch. . .

VINCE: Quit making excuses kid. Win some games. Did you ever hear, "winning isn't everything, it's…"

AARON: Yes, I know, it's the ONLY thing. You made that famous, Mr. Lombardi.

VINCE: Well, then get out there and get this thing fixed. I want to see you guys winning up there, got it?

AARON: Yes sir. But…aren't you… I mean, I thought you were…I mean, you keep saying "UP" there. Uh, which place are you, uh, calling from, exactly?

VINCE: From Milwaukee, kid. Where do you THINK I'm calling from, big shot, CHICAGO? It'll be a cold day in….

AARON: Okay, good, sir. Thanks for calling. We'll try to get things fixed for you, and…

VINCE: "Try" nothing — just DO it!

GUEST: A FREE AGENT – NO FOOLIN'!

AARON: Welcome back to another edition of "Aaron on the Air." So, let's see who we've got on line one.

BENNETT: Hey, Aaron. It's me. Martellus.

AARON: WHO?

BENNETT: Martellus Bennett, your new tight end.

ARRON: Hey, isn't somebody supposed to be screening these calls?!

BENNETT: No man, no prank, it's really me.

AARON: I remember you from the Bears. But then you want to the Patriots.

BENNETT: Yeah, I was — but Ted Thompson just signed me as a free agent.

AARON: Now I KNOW it's a prank call. Ted Thomson doesn't sign many free agents.

BENNETT; Well, he did THIS year. In fact, he signed four of us.

AARON: Bill Belichek is going to miss you, that's for sure.

BENNETT: Yeah, but I'm a Packer now. And Thompson really did sign four free agents including me!

AARON: You must be injured — or desperate. What'd he offer you, $25 and an old, rusty pickup truck?

BENNETT: Nope. $21 million over three years.

AARON: Wow. OK. So, I'll catch you later, Martellus.

BENNETT: No — I'll catch ***YOU*** later — maybe about eight times a game!

From Pitching Footballs to Pitching Stuff

AARON: Hi, this A-rod, host of the "Aaron on the Air" – the radio show where we take calls from VIPS. Especially "Very Important Packers.". Hello, caller, you're first in line.

BRETT: Hey, Aaron, how y'all doin'?

AARON: Sounds familiar — is this who I THINK it is?

BRETT: Yep, it is, but don't worry — I ain't coming back.

AARON: Brett Favre! Hey, man, good to talk to you. I mean, sort of...

BRETT: "Sort of?" Whaddya mean, aren't we cool, rookie?

AARON: See, it's things like that. You never treated me very well, and now, I'm one of the best QBs in the league.

BRETT: Aw, don't take it so seriously. I mean, I let you hold my clipboard, didn't I?

AARON: Yeah, but you were supposed to mentor me, and you gave me pretty bad advice.

BRETT: Bad advice? C'mon, man...

AARON: Like, you said "Talk back in meetings, coach loves it."

BRETT: Well, yeah, that...

AARON: And you tried to trick me. You said "don't worry about coverage – just pretend the defenders aren't there. Throw it anyway."

BRETT: What do you mean trick you? That's how I played, partner.

AARON: Okay, I guess it put you in the Hall of Fame, gunslinger.

AARON: Now, why'd you call my show?

BRETT: Got some more good advice for you, A-Rod. Copper Fit.

AARON: Oh, that brace thing? I've seen those ads with you.

BRETT: It's magic. Just go to www.dot...

AARON: (INTERRUPTING) Hey, now, no commercial plugs on my show.

BRETT: Oh, okay, then, I'll just hang up, slip in to my rugged, comfortable Wrangler jeans.

AARON: You did it again! Cool it with the commercial plugs. And, hey, what do you mean slip into them. What are you wearing…? OH, WAIT, NEVER MIND, DON'T ANSWER THAT.

BRETT: (EVIL LAUGH) Heh, heh, heh. Same thing I'll be wearing at your Hall of Fame induction speech a few years down the line. See you, buddy!

JAY "2-12 ALL-TIME VS. THE PACK" CUTLER

AARON: I'm Aaron Rodgers, and today's episode of "Aaron on the Air" features a special guest that Packer fans always looked forward to playing against: It's Jay Cutler, former Bears' quarterback and now Fox TV color analyst. Hello, Jay – how are you?

AARON: (AFTER SEVERAL MOMENTS OF SILENCE) Jay? Are you there?

CUTLER: I shrugged. Didn't you hear me shrug?

AARON: No, radio doesn't work that way.

CUTLER: Oh, yeah. Well, whatever....

AARON: Jay, you were cut by the Bears after a rocky career in Chicago. Fans complained that you just didn't care. How does that make you feel?

CUTLER: I don't care.

AARON: They also noticed your poor body language. Any reaction to that?

CUTLER: Yeah, I got some body language for them right HERE.

AARON: Uh, OK: I think we're lucky this IS radio. So let's instead talk about your FOX TV gig on NFL games.

CUTLER: (TOTALLY FLAT) I've never been so excited in my life.

AARON: Cool it, Jay: you don't have to be sarcastic.

CUTLER: No, I meant it. I'm excited.

AARON: Wow, really? Are you sure?.

CUTLER: Oh yeah? I'm sure about one thing — I've got some body language here for you, too.

AARON: Ohhhhhh-kay......GLAD we're on seven—second delay......I don't think that last comment by Jay made it on the air.....and we're out of time. Join us again next time on "Aaron on the Air."

Trivia Teasers

Did You Know?

▶ Packer Nation

Green Bay is the NFL's smallest market with a metro population of 306,241, which is easily surpassed by the number of Packers' backers who are members of Facebook (4.4 million fans) and Twitter (701,000 fans).

▶ Packer Pro Shop ('Till You Drop!)

Long ago, the Packer Pro Shop used to be the size of a phone booth. That was then, this is now — given it's now a gargantuan 21,500 square feet and stocked with amazing "stocking stuffer" gifts for a grandma and a grandson near you. The place is popular: Shopping carts were added at the front door recently for your shopping pleasure.

▶ When were the Green Bay Packers founded?

Answer: August 11, 1919.
The Green Bay Packers were founded by Curly Lambeau and George Whitney Calhoun. The Packers were a semi-professional team from 1919-1920.

▶ Which NFL Team had the first cheerleaders?

Answer: Green Bay Packers.
Also known as the Golden Girls, they led the Packers fans in cheers from 1961 to 1972.

▶ In what round of the 1956 draft was QB Bart Starr selected?

Answer: 17th. Starr was selected 200th overall out of Alabama.

▶ In their first season, where did the Packers play their home games?

Answer: Hagemeister Park.
Hagemeister Park had no bleachers so the fans could roam around freely. There were ropes along side of the field so the

fans would not enter it. During halftime, the teams would meet in opposite endzones to make plays, and fans would sometimes enter the conversations. To pay the players, they would pass around a hat to collect donations from fans. The Packers played six total games in the 1919 season at Hagemeister Park.

- **In 1929, the Packers won their first NFL Championship. Undefeated, they finished with a 12-0-1 record (including one tie). How many of their 13 games did the Packers shut out their opponents?**

  Answer: Eight.
  With an amazing defense, the Packers allowed only 22 points in the season. This included their only tie, 0-0, against the Frankford Yellow Jackets in week 11. The Packers would go on to be the first team to win three consecutive NFL Championships, winning again in 1930 and 1931. The franchise would later duplicate this by winning three again from 1965-1967.

- **To whom did Brett Favre complete his first career NFL pass?**

  Answer: Favre.
  Favre caught his own deflected pass and was tackled immediately, resulting in a loss of seven yards.

- **Thanks Paul**

  During the 1961 NFL season, running back Paul Hornung was called up for active service in the United States Army. He was able to get weekend passes to continue playing football, including one approved by President John F. Kennedy (a friend of coach Vince Lombardi) to play in the 1961 Championship Game against the New York Giants.

▶ **In the 1980 season, which Packer turned a blocked kick into a sudden death victory for the team?**

Answer: Chester Marcol.
On September 7, 1980, Marcol's field goal attempt against the Chicago Bears was blocked, but the ball bounded back into his arms. Marcol scampered 25 yards for a TD, giving the Packers a 12-6 overtime victory.

▶ **Where did the name "Packers" originate?**

The name comes from its first sponsor, the Indian Packing Company, which in 1919 gave $500 to employee Curly Lambeau for uniforms and equipment for the football team he founded. A year later, Indian was purchased by the Acme Packing Company, which continued to support the team. So the Packers have, since their formation, been a nod to the canned meatpacking industry that helped launch them.

PACKER PUNCHLINES

- The Cowboys yearn to finally win another Super Bowl, so what's their new slogan?

  Answer: Make America's Team Great Again.

- In Seattle, the "12th Man" is a symbol of pride among fans. What is the "12th Man" in San Francisco?

  Answer: The number left watching the team by the 4th quarter.

- What do all the Vikings' best-ever superstars have in common?

  Answer: AARP memberships.

- At the end of the season, while the Packers are playing for championships, what are the Lions, Bears and Vikings playing for?

  Answer: Their professional lives.

- What's the most popular Lions T-shirt slogan?

  Answer: The Lions are gonna WIN this year! (At least once.)

- Does Jay Cutler have the voice to be a Fox analyst?

  Answer: No one knows – he's always spoken only in body language.

- How does Bears' coach John Fox start every quarterback meeting?

  Answer: Same way the last four coaches did: "I forgot. Tell me your name again?"

- What does Dez Bryant enjoy more than making cornerbacks pay?

  Answer: Making teammates pay when they go out for dinner.

- During that famous "Fail Mary" game against Seattle, what did the refs have in common with players who were out injured?

  Answer: They both missed a great game.

- Will Marshawn Lynch talk to reporters now that he's back?

  Answer: No – but he'll be ignoring a whole new batch in Oakland.

- Hear about the new uniform for Lions' secondary?

  Answer: Comes with an extra jockstrap since they get faked out of theirs so often.

- While Tom Brady apparently believes in deflation before games, what does Aaron Rogers prefer?

  Answer: R-E-L-A-X ation.

- Brett Favre says he can play in the NFL until he's 80? Is he correct?

  Answer: You mean he didn't?????

- What did Pete Carroll say upon leaving as USC head coach for the same job with the Seahawks?

  Answer: "I leave behind a great bunch of friends, colleagues, and allegations."

- Why do the Packers love playing Thursday night games?

  Answer: Only four days from one victory to the next.

- Who do you have to talk to get a Packer season ticket if you're way down the waiting list?

  Answer: God. But he's only 36 spots ahead of you.

- What sells better than hot dogs and beer at Lions' preseason games?

  Answer: No-Doz.

- Why do Packer fans in Green Bay want the team to play regular season games in Milwaukee again?

  Answer: Better weather. Better beer.

- Why do all the NFC North's teams besides Green Bay have cheerleading squads?

  Answer: Beats watching the performance of the home team.

- Remember that one-year backup QB Jim McMahon who wore his Bear's jersey to the White House celebration?

  Answer: Us either.

- Why do Bears' fans think about their 1986 Super Bowl victory so much?

  Answer: It's either that or Jay Cutler. What would YOU do?

- Do some people really think there's too much football on TV?

  Answer: Yes — mostly fans of the Bears, Lions, and Vikings.

- Does Jerry Jones really charge $27.50 per ticket for a guided tour of AT&T Stadium during the offseason?

  Answer: Yes — but that's because they don't have to watch the Cowboys play.

- And does he really charge $89 per vehicle for premium parking at the stadium?

  Answer: Yes — and Dez Bryant expects a tip after parking your car, too.

- Do you think Jim Harbaugh misses coaching the 49ers?

  Answer: No — he still gets to coach players with college-level talent.

- Why do the Cowboys and 49ers always wear solid-color uniforms?

  Answer: Provides a better contrast with their checkered pasts.

- What do the Lions' players say at practice when ordered to "lineup"?

  Answer: "Wait — I haven't even been fingerprinted yet!"

- What are "two-a-days" for the Lions?

  Answer: The maximum number of times linemen are allowed to visit Burger King.

- When cheerleaders of the Vikings, Lions, and Bears as the crowd to "make some noise" what do the fans do?

  Answer: Snore louder.

- They say renovations made Soldier Field look like a spaceship. That figures, since their players always seem to be on another planet.

- Why does the Army call enemy communications systems "Cutlers"?

  Answer: Because their messages are so easy to intercept.

- Why does Burger King's new promotion feature Jay Cutler?

  Answer: Because you get to "pick six" items for $5.

- To make losing 49er fans feel better, tell them one stat their team is leading the league in: penalties

- What's the best way for a Viking fan to watch his team win a Super Bowl?

  Answer: Don't pick any Vikings for his fantasy team.

- During the Lions' 0-16 season, why didn't they see the fans with bags over their heads?

  Answer: Because they were wearing them, too.

- Next to Lambeau Field, the design of the "Titletown District" features stores, restaurants, a hotel, and more fun. What was it first called before "Titletown District" was chosen?

  Answer: Lombardi Land.

- The Packers wear "throw-back jerseys" that hearken to the past. The Bears wear "throw-up jerseys," given the team's performance is hard for their fans to swallow.

- What does the Bears' head coach truly mean when he says his quarterback is a great game manager?

  Answer: "He throws too many interceptions, so we hope our running game saves us."

- What does the 49ers' coach truly mean when he says "we play 'em one at a time?"

  Answer: "Which is too bad, since I'd love to get them all over with at once."

- What does the Giants' GM truly mean when he says his latest draft pick was "chosen for his potential?"

  Answer: "Well, we had to pick somebody."

- Can you predict how long until the roof on the Viking's new U.S. Bank Stadium caves in like the roof of the Metrodome did in 2010?

  Answer: No, but the roof caves in on the Viking's season pretty much every year.

- How do you know a Bears' draft pick will ride the bench all season?

  Answer: Because he's a Bears' draft pick.

- Why do the Lions never oversleep?

  Answer: Because every bad performance is "a wake-up call."

- The Vikings look far and wide for kickers. But the ones they sign kick field goals the same way: far and WIDE.

- When a Cowboy says "We've got our backs against the wall now," what does he truly mean?

  Answer: He's probably calling from the police station.

- What does the 49ers' announcer truly mean when saying the team's QB has "happy feet"?

  Answer: He's happy he didn't get killed, thanks to his horrible offensive line.

- How mad were Seahawk players at Pete Carroll for calling a pass that was intercepted on the 1-yard line in the Super Bowl?

  Answer: They bought him bath toys for the holidays: a toaster and radio.

- Jay Cutler said he always gave 100% as Bears' quarterback: 15% each weekday, 20% on Saturdays, 5% on Sundays.

- What do the Packer players truly mean when saying "you can throw out all the records" before playing the Bears?

  Answer: "We don't need records — we'll be listening to our iPhones on the bench by halftime once we put this game out of reach."

- The Vikings are rethinking the glass roof on their new stadium after they were booed from the International Space Station.

- How are the Seahawks like the military?

  Answer: They always bring the "heavy artillery" to games, then, afterward, act like loose cannons.

- What happens when Chris Christie is alone in the Cowboys' skybox?

  Answer: Standing Room Only.

- What would make the Bears more entertaining to watch on TV?

  Answer: A laugh track.

- Lacking offensive firepower, the Lions' running backs are hoping to hit paydirt more often this season. Then they'll be able to demand more than dirt pay.

- Cowboys' receivers are lousy at running "up and out" routes, but they are great at having "down and out" seasons.

- It's sad, but Tony Romo gets injured so often, he passes out the same statement to the media every year. What does it say?

  Answer: "IR on IR again."

- How do female Browns fans describe their "bust" size?

  Answer: Tim Couch, Brady Quinn, Johnny Manziel, or Brandon Weedon.

- The Giants' GM was asked how long it would take for his team to rebuild.
  His answer: "When did you say Haley's Comet will return?"

- At cut-down time, immature Seahawks know the gig is up on their playing career when an assistant coach summons them by saying: "The GM wants to see you. . . and bring your comic books."

- Give the Cowboys credit for acting like their namesake. Every year they are saddled with unrealistic expectations, and they play like what their horses leave behind.

- An approaching new season activates eternal optimism in Bears fans: jump merely three spots in the standings and your team wins its division.

- Jerry Jones favorite song by Frank Sinatra reminds him of the Cowboys: "I blew it my way."

- When the Vikings finally win the Super Bowl, which kind of t-shirts sell out first?

  Answer: XXXXL

- Expanding the season to 18 games has the Lions worried. After going 0-16 in 2008, no one wants to take any chances on beating their own infamous record.

- Calling Eli Manning "Mr. September" sounds perfect because he's usually never playing in January.

- Expanding the playoffs to include more teams with perpetual mediocre records has its advocates, including the Cowboys' Jerry Jones.

- In contrast to the Packers' second-half victory comebacks, what kind of comebacks are typical for Richard Sherman?

  Answer: Snarky ones.

- What's the only kind of ring Vikings' players will ever wear?

  Answer: Wedding.

- What's the favorite word announcers use in combination with "veteran" to describe Jay Cutler?

  Answer: Embattled.

- Where's the most likely place for the 49ers to find an MVP?

  Answer: The other sideline.

- When the Lions win three in a row, what chant do you hear from their fans?

  Answer: We'll let you know if it ever happens.

- Why do NFC North teams never play exhibition games vs. Green Bay?

  Answer: Three losses during one season is one more than necessary.

- Mention 1986 to Bears' fans, and they immediately remember "Super Bowl win." Mention that year to other fans and what do they think?

  Answer: and what do they think? Hey, were dinosaurs around then?

- Will Jay Cutler enjoy life as a broadcaster?

  Answer: Yes – he won't have to walk quickly to his car anymore after home games.

- What's the difference between 2 and 21 to Bears' fans?

  Answer: 2 = the number of consecutive Packer Hall of Fame quarterbacks and 21 is the number of consecutive Bears' quarterbacks certain to NEVER make the Hall of Fame.

- What's strange about the penalty for speeding in Illinois?

  Answer: You receive a Bears' ticket. . . two if it's a second offense.

- When you hear the announcer describing a Lions' player as a "wily veteran," you can be sure he's talking about who?

  Answer: The fans favorite player: the backup quarterback.

- Why is stepping into a Walmart like visiting Soldier Field?

  Answer: It's where you're sure to find a loss leader.

- How do you know downtrodden losers such as Cleveland, Jacksonville, and Tennessee will finally attract an enthusiastic, sellout crowd?

  Answer: The Packers will come to town.

- Why did they call Jay Cutler an "old school" quarterback?

  Answer: He always telegraphed his passes.

- You know the Lions' coach thinks one of his players should retire when he says what?

  Answer: "He gives back a lot to the community. I wish to hell he'd join it."

- Now that Jay Cutler has retired, Chicago bakeries can once again compete for the "most turnovers" made on a Sunday.

- What did the Vikings save a lot of money on by building a domed stadium?

  Answer: Sideline heaters.

- A-Rod wants Packer fans to R-E-L-A-X. Bear players want their fans to give them a little R-E-S-P-E-C-T.

- In free agency, why do the Vikings always court a player by flying their corporate jet to meet him in some exotic location?

  Answer: In winter, the only "lure" in Minnesota is used in ice fishing.

- Pete Carroll paces the sidelines with such gusto, he looks like he's looking for a rest room.

- Richard Sherman is so full of himself, he hardly ever gets hungry.

- How badly have the Bears played?

  Answer: They got suspended for taking NON-performance enhancing drugs.

- Which four quarterbacks are the best choices for the Packer Hall Of Fame (based on the amazing number of victories they produced for the the team)?

  Answer: Bart Starr, Brett Favre, Aaron Rodgers, and Jay Cutler.

▶ REMEMBER THE TIME?:

Matt Flynn subbed for A-Rod on New Year's Day and threw for six touchdowns and 480 yards — then spent the rest of his career proving that he was NOT A-Rod? (His final career totals stand at 17 touchdowns and 2,541 yards for eight years in the league — INCLUDING the big six TD game!)

▶ REMEMBER THE TIME?:

Early in his coaching career, Packer coach Mike McCarthy had a part-time job working on the Pennsylvania Turnpike in the toll booth? Rumor has it that's where he first figured out how to use the "nickel back."

▶ REMEMBER THE TIME?:

McCarthy helped Ricky Williams rush for more than 2,200 yards and 14 TD's for New Orleans. (He says he doesn't want to take all the credit — it was a joint effort.)

▶ REMEMBER THE TIME?:

In 2008, when the Packers had a rotten year at 6-10, and they still finished SIX GAMES ahead of the Detroit Lions?

- Bears' legendary coach Mike Ditka saw his role on ESPN's football pregame show reduced dramatically after he strongly announced that he was backing Donald Trump for president. No one has disappeared that quickly since his Bears' string of quick playoff exits after winning the Super Bowl in January, 1986.

- Bears fans were not happy in 2016 when the team waived long-time kicker and fan-favorite Robbie Gould. Turns out his replacement was not as good as Gould.

- Jay Cutler's 2016 thumb injury cost him many games as backup Brian Hoyer played well (before himself getting injured with a broken left arm). While riding the bench, Jay responded with sagging shoulders, a pouty attitude, poor language, and a foul disposition — so it appears that being replaced in the lineup did not affect him in any way.

- Shoe stores in Minneapolis carry shoes in narrow, regular, "wide left" or "wide right" depending upon your favorite Vikings placekicker. (Which is still confusing, because missing wide left or wide right is still pretty "regular" for the Vikings!)

About The Author

Mike Marn's LOL humor has been enjoyed by thousands who have attended his stand-up gigs, chuckled at his greeting cards, snickered at his magazine columns, and, even, giggled along with Pat S. and the Wheel of Fortune audience.

Mike's "Everyman" Resume includes wearing a college professor's hat and an ad agency creative director cap.

Share Your Own Packer Poems & Punchlines At packerjokes.com

We'll pick the best ones and post them at **packerjokes.com**.

Check back at the site later to see if you won the contest among others that submit.

Of course, feel free to tell your friends about **packerjokes.com** where they can:

1) see samples from the book
2) order the book
3) submit their own Packer poems and punchlines

76281719R00065

Made in the USA
Columbia, SC
04 September 2017